DINOSAURS ALL AROUND

AN ARTIST'S VIEW OF THE PREHISTORIC WORLD

BY **CAROLINE ARNOLD**

PHOTOGRAPHS BY **RICHARD HEWETT**

CLARION BOOKS

NEW YORK

CLARION BOOKS
a Houghton Mifflin Company imprint
215 Park Avenue South, New York, NY 10003
Text copyright © 1993 by Caroline Arnold
Photographs copyright © 1993 by Richard Hewett

Photo Credits: Stephen and Sylvia Czerkas, pages 18 and 21.

Book designed by Sylvia Frezzolini.

Printed in Singapore.

Library of Congress Cataloging-in-Publication Data

Arnold, Caroline.
Dinosaurs all around: an artist's view of the prehistoric world / by Caroline Arnold ;
photographs by Richard Hewett.
p.   cm.
Summary: On a visit to the workshop of Stephen and Sylvia Czerkas where a life-size
dinosaur is being constructed, the reader learns much information about dinosaurs and
how conclusions are made from fossil remains.
ISBN 0-395-62363-4   PA ISBN 0-395-86620-0
1. Dinosaurs–Models–Design and construction–Juvenile literature. 2. Dinosaurs–
Juvenile literature. [1. Dinosaurs–Models–Design and construction. 2. Dinosaurs]
I. Hewett, Richard, ill. II. Title.
QE862.D5A752 1993
567.9'1–dc20   92-5726
                                                                          CIP
                                                                          AC

TWP 10 9 8 7 6 5 4

Stephen and Sylvia Czerkas with life-size *Compsognathus* sculpture.

ACKNOWLEDGMENTS

For their enthusiastic participation in this project and gracious hospitality we are extremely grateful to Sylvia and Stephen Czerkas. We also thank Ellen Girardeau, Mary Ann Dunn, and Cecile Fisher at the Natural History Museum of Los Angeles County in California, and Janet Dean and the staff of the Museum of Northern Arizona, Flagstaff, Arizona, for their cooperation. For their assistance with the photographs we thank Cecile Fisher, Lin, Sasha, and Jasper Sircus, Adam Forner, and Andrea Aluiller.

Most of the dinosaur models pictured in this book were part of two traveling museum exhibits, "Dinosaurs Past and Present" and "Dinosaurs: A Global View," which were sponsored by the Natural History Museum of Los Angeles County. The first was curated by Sylvia Czerkas and the second was created by Czerkas Studios. Stephen Czerkas's work can also be seen in the permanent collections of the Natural History Museum of Los Angeles County, the California Academy of Sciences, the New Mexico Museum of Natural History, the Philadelphia Academy of Sciences, the Tyrrell Museum of Paleontology in Alberta, and elsewhere.

All dinosaur sculptures photographed for this book are by Stephen Czerkas except for the *Stegosaurus* (page 40) by Charles Knight and the baby *Protoceratops* (page 43) by Sylvia Czerkas.

What did dinosaurs really look like? How big were they, what did they eat, and how did they move? Scientists ask these questions because they want to know what life was like hundreds of millions of years ago when dinosaurs roamed the earth. People who make paintings and sculptures of dinosaurs also want to know the answers so they can accurately depict these animals in their artwork. Their representations help us to understand better what life was like in that ancient world.

Dinosaur Hall, Natural History Museum of Los Angeles County. Left to right: life-size model of *Allosaurus, Diplodocus* skeleton, and *Stegosaurus* skeleton.

In his studio, Stephen Czerkas peers into the giant jaw of his partially finished *Carnotaurus* sculpture.

MAKING DINOSAURS

Stephen Czerkas (pronounced CHER-kus) is a sculptor who specializes in making realistic life-size models of dinosaurs. He has created dozens of dinosaur models that are exhibited in museums all over the world. The colors, textures, and action poses of his dinosaur sculptures make them seem so real that you can imagine them stepping off their platforms and wandering around the exhibit hall.

Stephen Czerkas has been fascinated with dinosaurs all his life. He made his first dinosaur sculpture with mud in his back yard when he was four years old. As he grew older he read about dinosaurs, drew pictures of them, and made many original models. He even made a short film using his own dinosaurs. When he grew up his first job was making movable models of monsters and other animals that were used to create special effects in movies. In the movie business Stephen learned many of the techniques that he now uses to make dinosaur models for museums.

Stephen's wife, Sylvia, is also an artist and is his partner. She has made her own dinosaur models in the past but now works with Stephen. Together they have written several books about dinosaurs. Sylvia has also organized three large dinosaur exhibits for museums.

Stephen moves the head of *Allosaurus.*

Finished 1/10 scale model of *Carnotaurus*.

Getting Started

Artists who make drawings or sculptures of ancient life forms are called paleoartists. ("Paleo" is a Greek word meaning "ancient.") Paleontologists are scientists who study the remains of ancient plants and animals. Stephen Czerkas is both a paleoartist and a paleontologist. To learn everything he can about dinosaurs he reads scientific papers, consults with other paleontologists, and goes to museums to study their dinosaur collections. He and Sylvia also go on fossil-hunting expeditions both near their home in Utah and around the world.

Stephen usually begins a dinosaur project by making small sculptures. For these he uses a soft modeling clay like Plasticene, and attaches it to a wire framework called an armature. Both the clay and the wire are flexible, so Stephen can experiment with putting the dinosaur in various poses. These first sculptures are done quickly and, like the sketches an artist does in preparation for a large painting, they help Stephen develop ideas that he can use later in his large finished models. Sometimes Stephen also makes small-scale models that are finished pieces of art. These are completed in the same way that he would do a life-size piece.

Stephen begins work on a small clay sculpture.

The largest dinosaur Stephen has ever made is a life-size model of *Carnotaurus* (kar-no-TOR-us) that measures 14 feet high and 28 feet long. It is based on a nearly complete skeleton that was discovered in the 1980s on a remote ranch in southern Argentina. The name *Carnotaurus*, which means "meat-eating bull," refers to the bull-like horns on its forehead.

Carnotaurus lived in South America about 100 million years ago, a time when the landmasses of North and South America were not connected. Stephen's sculpture will help people to understand some of the similarities and differences between Northern and Southern Hemisphere dinosaurs at that time. For instance, in North America, *Tyrannosaurus rex* (ty-RAN-uh-SOR-us rex) was the dominant meat eater, whereas in South America, the best-known carnivore was *Carnotaurus*. The back legs of *Carnotaurus* were large and sturdy, like those of *Tyrannosaurus rex*, but its forelimbs were much shorter so they were more limited in their use.

Stephen's studio provides him with plenty of space to work plus room for tools and sculpting materials. Scaffolding helps Stephen reach the upper parts of a large dinosaur.

Bones and Skeletons

When a fossilized dinosaur skeleton is found, the bones are usually scattered and some are missing. Identifying them and putting them together is like solving a large jigsaw puzzle. To figure out how to assemble the bones of a dinosaur skeleton, scientists compare them to other fossil bones and to the bones in skeletons of modern animals.

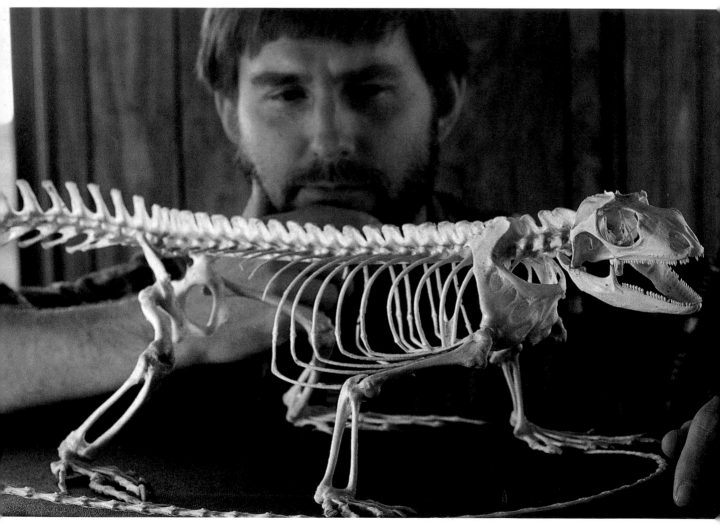

Stephen studies the skeleton of an iguana, a modern reptile.

Part of the cast of a *Carnotaurus* skeleton.

In a living animal, the bones of the skeleton form a framework that supports the rest of the body, just as the metal armature supports a clay sculpture. Bones also protect the inner body organs and provide surfaces to which muscles can attach. The sizes and textures of the bones help reveal the shape of these muscles. Whenever possible, Stephen Czerkas likes to use casts, or copies, of actual bones as the basis for his life-size sculptures. Then, by adding the muscles on top of the bones, he can build the animal from the inside out.

Building the Body

In the same way that an architect draws blueprints for a building, Stephen makes many drawings for each of the dinosaurs he sculpts. Every part must be carefully measured and drawn to scale so that the finished animal is the correct size and has the right proportions. Although Stephen does most of the building and sculpting, Sylvia helps him with the detail work.

For a large dinosaur such as *Carnotaurus*, Stephen first makes a strong steel support to hold the skeleton. Then he builds up the animal's body with a special oil base clay. Because this kind of clay does not harden, Stephen can work with it as long as necessary until the shape of each part is just right. For the surface of his sculptures, Stephen uses a different type of clay that is better for revealing fine detail.

(Left) Checking the plan for *Carnotaurus*.

(Right) Sculpting the leg of *Carnotaurus*.

Dinosaur Skin

Like reptiles today, dinosaurs had scaly skin. Modern reptiles such as snakes and most lizards have flat, overlapping scales. Dinosaurs had small, bumpy knobs called "tubercles" that were arranged in circular patterns. The skin pattern of each species had a distinctive shape and design. Like fingerprints, these patterns help identify the kind of dinosaur to which a piece of skin belonged. The size and pattern of the scales also varied with their location on the body. In areas where the skin folded or needed to be flexible, the scales were smaller than on flatter areas. Although dinosaur skin fossils are not as common as fossil bones, there are samples from many species, and these provide a guide for dinosaur artists.

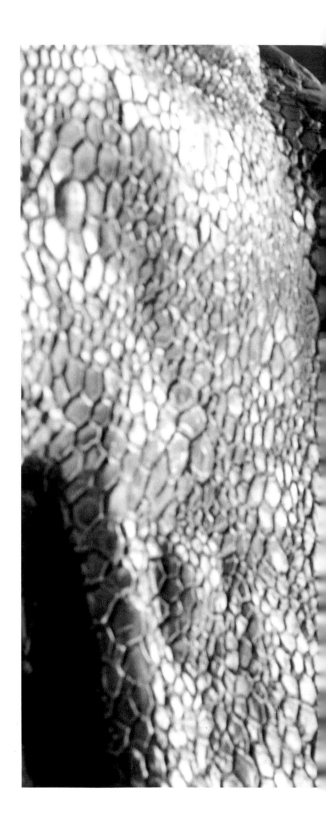

The skin of *Styracosaurus* had a rosette pattern.

Stephen specializes in studying skin impressions of dinosaurs. Here he helps collect *Carnotaurus* skin fossils in Argentina.

Sometimes paleontologists find fossilized impressions of dinosaur skin in the same places that they find fossil dinosaur bones. The skin itself rotted away millions of years ago, but its texture was pressed into soft mud that later became stone. One of the most important examples of dinosaur skin fossils came with the discovery of the *Carnotaurus* skeleton in Argentina. Stephen often makes plaster casts of such fossils. In some cases he is able to press a thin sheet of clay against the casts to get an exact copy of the skin to use on his sculptures. After pressing the clay skin segments to the dinosaur's body Stephen smooths the edges together and adds missing details.

(Above) The plaster cast shows the dinosaur's skin pattern in reverse.

(Below) Stephen attaches a small piece of clay skin to the leg of his *Carnotaurus* sculpture.

Casting the Body

The clay dinosaurs that Stephen makes in his studio are the first step in creating a finished model for a museum. Because the clay remains soft, these sculptures are not good for exhibition pieces. The clay is also very heavy. So Stephen makes copies of his sculptures out of lighter-weight, more permanent materials.

In the same way that a model airplane is put together from tiny parts, a dinosaur model is also constructed of many pieces. To make the pieces for the dinosaur model, Stephen divides the clay dinosaur sculpture into many sections. Then he paints each section with a liquid rubber called latex, layering it with cheese-cloth for extra strength. As the latex dries, it takes on the exact shape of the clay surface.

When the latex is dry, Stephen paints liquid fiberglass over it. The fiberglass hardens and creates a rigid support for the latex so the latex can be used as a mold. At this point the mold can be removed from the dinosaur. It is an exact copy of the dinosaur in reverse.

(Left) Before the molds are made, the sculpture must be checked and measured to make sure that everything is accurate.

(Below) Removing the molds from the clay sculpture of *Allosaurus*.

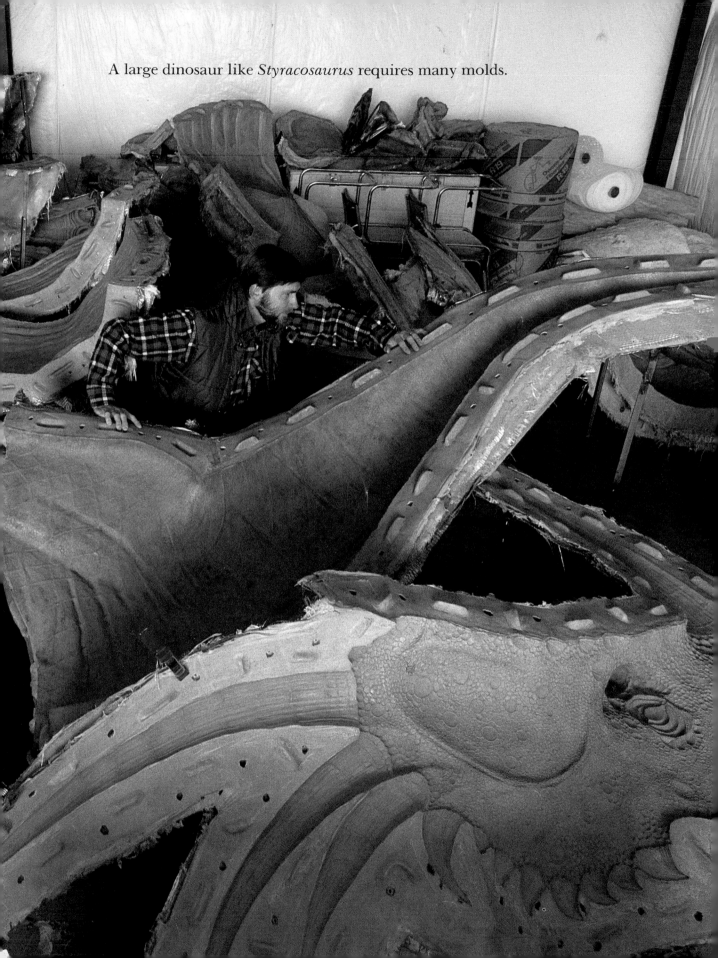

A large dinosaur like *Styracosaurus* requires many molds.

The mold is removed from the cast of a *Carnotaurus* bone.

The cast of each part of the dinosaur is made by pouring resin, a kind of liquid plastic, into the mold. Fiberglass and steel are added for strength and the resin is allowed to harden. When the mold is removed, the resin has formed a sturdy and exact copy of that part of the original sculpture. The molds can be used over and over to make many dinosaurs. Once the molds have been made, there is no more need for the clay sculpture. It can be destroyed and the clay reused to make a new dinosaur.

Making the molds and casting each section may take many weeks. Finally, when all the parts are cast, the pieces are assembled and the dinosaur model is ready to be painted.

What Colors Were Dinosaurs?

Although we can make good guesses about the colors of dinosaurs, we will never know for sure exactly how they were marked. In choosing how to paint his dinosaur models, Stephen considers the animal's age, size, and behavior, as well as the environment in which it lived. Young dinosaurs probably had drab, earthy colors that would have helped conceal them from

The colors of this *Deinonychus* are similar to those of a modern leopard.

predators. Predatory dinosaurs, like tigers or leopards today, might have had stripes or spots that would have helped them hide while they waited to pounce on their victims. Animals that lived in groups might have had distinctive patterns to help individuals recognize one another. Although some dinosaurs may have had dull-colored skin, others may have been brightly marked just as some birds and reptiles are today.

(Above) Museum staff unload a dinosaur crate from the truck.

(Right) *Deinonychus* emerges from its packing crate.

At the Museum

When the last drops of paint are dry, the dinosaur model is finally ready for delivery. Specially designed packing crates hold each dinosaur safely while it is being transported. Then, when it arrives at the museum, the crate is carefully unloaded and the dinosaur is carried or rolled into the exhibit hall. Stephen mounts each large piece on wheels to make it easier to handle both when he is working on it and when it is being installed at a museum.

A large dinosaur model, such as *Styracosaurus* (sty-RAK-uh-SOR-us), weighs nearly a ton and is too big to travel in one piece. Stephen constructed it in parts so that it could be easily assembled after it arrived at the museum.

In real life *Styracosaurus* had strong neck muscles that held its huge head onto its body. For his sculpture, Stephen designed a steel support that allowed the head and neck to slide into place. In a dramatic moment recorded by the local news media, Stephen and the museum staff attached the *Styracosaurus* head. After the head was securely fastened and the other parts of the exhibit had been installed, the dinosaurs were finally ready for public view.

Styracosaurus is assembled.

Life-size *Styracosaurus* model.

AMAZING DINOSAURS

People first learned about dinosaurs when a large fossilized tooth was found in England in 1822. It belonged to a dinosaur called *Iguanodon* (ih-GWAN-uh-don), a lizard-like reptile that was 30 feet long and weighed about 4 tons. *Iguanodon* was also the subject for the first life-size dinosaur model. When it was finished, twenty-two men sat inside it and had a dinner party!

Ever since the first dinosaur discovery, people have wanted to know more about these giant beasts that roamed the earth hundreds of millions of years ago. Scientists divide the dinosaur age into three periods—the Triassic, from 248 to 213 million years ago; the Jurassic, from 213 to 144 million years ago; and the most recent period, the Cretaceous, which lasted from 144 to 65 million years ago. Dinosaurs first appeared in the late Triassic period, about 225 million years ago, and they became extinct at the end of the Cretaceous period. Hundreds of different kinds of dinosaurs lived during this 160-million-year span. Stephen Czerkas's models help us to learn how some of these dinosaurs may have looked and how they might have lived.

Styracosaurus

Styracosaurus was a large dinosaur that lived about 90 million years ago in North America and Asia. It was nearly 20 feet long and 10 feet high. This stoutly built animal ate plants and, like buffalo in modern times, moved about in large herds. Its strong beak-like mouth would have been good for breaking off tough leaves and stalks.

Styracosaurus, which means "spike reptile," was one of the ceratopsian, or horn-faced, dinosaurs. The dinosaurs in this group, which includes *Triceratops* (try-SAIR-uh-tops) and *Protoceratops* (proh-tuh-SAIR-uh-tops), had various kinds of horns and bony shields on their heads and necks, like built-in armor. These dinosaurs may have used their horns as defense against predators or in battles with one another. The ceratopsian dinosaurs also had powerful tail muscles.

Skull of *Albertosaurus*.

Albertosaurus

As with animals in today's world, dinosaurs adopted a wide variety of lifestyles. Some, like the ceratopsian dinosaurs, were plant eaters, or herbivores. Others were meat eaters, or carnivores. Predators of *Styracosaurus* and other plant-eating animals of the Cretaceous period would have included *Albertosaurus* (al-BER-tuh-SOR-us), a large meat-eating dinosaur named after Alberta, Canada, the place where its fossil

Face of *Albertosaurus*.

bones were found. *Albertosaurus* had huge jaws lined with enormous sharp teeth and feet armed with strong, sharp claws. Stephen Czerkas's life-size sculpture of an *Albertosaurus* head is modeled over the cast of a fossil skull. He decided to leave half of the skull exposed to show viewers the relationship of the muscles to the bones. The head measures more than 40 inches long and 33 inches high. The entire animal grew to a length of 28 feet, was 13 feet tall, and weighed 2.5 tons.

(Above) *Tyrannosaurus rex* (1/10 scale).

(Right) *Tyrannosaurus rex* had a large head and powerful jaws.

Tyrannosaurus rex

A relative of *Albertosaurus* was *Tyrannosaurus rex*, the biggest and most fearsome meat-eating dinosaur of all. *Tyrannosaurus rex*, whose name means "tyrant reptile king," grew to a length of 45 feet and weighed up to 7.5 tons.

For many years, this heavily built dinosaur was pictured standing upright with its long tail dragging on the ground. Now, as scientists have learned more about how this giant moved and behaved, they believe that the usual walking position of *Tyrannosaurus rex* was more likely horizontal, with its head lowered and the tail raised for balance. Stephen Czerkas's sculpture of *Tyrannosaurus rex* (1/10 scale) shows the new view of its posture.

Allosaurus

During the Jurassic period the largest meat-eating dinosaur was *Allosaurus*. It lived in western North America and preyed on animals such as *Apatosaurus* (ah-PAT-uh-SOR-us), also known as *Brontosaurus* (BRON-tuh-SOR-us), and *Diplodocus* (dih-PLOD-uh-kus), large dinosaurs that could be 80 or more feet long. Most allosaurs were about 23 feet in length, although a few fossils have been found of animals that were up to 39 feet long. Even though allosaurs were much smaller than some of the large dinosaurs they ate, they were successful hunters because they were powerful and quick. They walked on sturdy rear legs and had short forelimbs with three sharp-clawed fingers. Fossil tracks of allosaurs suggest that sometimes they might have hunted in groups.

Allosaurus had a large head with two bony ridges above its nose, and strong jaws and teeth that were well suited for ripping flesh. Like reptiles today, *Allosaurus* could not chew its food. Instead, it tore off chunks of flesh and swallowed them whole.

Fossil teeth provided examples
for those in the mouth of *Allosaurus*.

Deinonychus

Not all meat-eating dinosaurs were huge. *Deinonychus* (day-NON-ee-kus) was about 10 feet long and stood 3 to 5 feet tall. This agile and quick-moving dinosaur lived in western North America about 140 million years ago. Its fossil bones were first found in Montana in 1964. The name *Deinonychus* means "terrible claw" and refers to the long, sharp claws on the dinosaur's back feet. This dinosaur would have been able to leap on its victim, grasp it with its forelimbs, and use its back claws to slash through the skin. *Deinonychus* may have hunted in packs the same way that modern wolves do.

Compsognathus

The smallest meat eater was also the smallest known dinosaur. *Compsognathus* (komp-SOG-nath-us), which is pictured on the acknowledgments page, lived in the late Jurassic period. This dinosaur, whose name means "elegant jaw," was less than three feet long. It fed on insects, fish, and other small animals it found at the edges of the swamps where it lived. In southern Germany, a complete skeleton of *Compsognathus* was discovered along with the perfectly preserved skeleton of a small lizard curled up inside the cavity where the dinosaur's stomach had been. Evidently the dinosaur had eaten the lizard just before it died.

(Top left) *Deinonychus.*
(Below left) The sharp-clawed back foot of *Deinonychus.*

Stegosaurus

One of the most intriguing of North American dinosaurs is *Stegosaurus* (steg-uh-SOR-us), whose name means "plated reptile." It lived in what is now the western United States during the Jurassic period, grew to a length of 25 feet, and weighed up to 5 tons. This plant eater had a bony head, a thick body, a long tail, and a series of pointed plates along its back and tail. How these flat plates were positioned along *Stegosaurus*'s back has been a topic of much debate. For a long time, people thought they were in two rows, either paired or in an alternating pattern. Before making his model of *Stegosaurus*, Stephen Czerkas examined many fossil skeletons of this animal. He concluded that the most likely arrangement of the plates was along a single line with alternate plates slanting slightly outward on the shoulders and neck. Other scientists now agree that this is the way *Stegosaurus* probably looked. No one knows what purpose the plates may have served. Perhaps they were used for defense. Maybe they were used to impress other stegosaurs. Possibly they helped the stegosaur to regulate its body temperature.

On the left an old version of *Stegosaurus* sculpted by Charles Knight shows two rows of plates; on the right Stephen Czerkas's model of *Stegosaurus* has a single row of plates.

Dinosaur Eggs

Another question that intrigues dinosaur scientists is how dinosaur babies were born. Because dinosaurs were reptiles, scientists long suspected that they laid eggs just as modern reptiles do. However, the first dinosaur eggs were not discovered until 1923 when a nest was found in the Gobi desert in Mongolia. The eggs in it had been laid 100 million years earlier by the stout, horn-faced dinosaur called *Protoceratops*. The eggs and skeletons of newly hatched and young *Protoceratops* provided scientists with the first evidence of dinosaur growth and development.

Since the *Protoceratops* discovery, people have found eggs and nests of many other dinosaur species. One of the most spectacular finds was of a huge nesting ground of a duckbill dinosaur called *Maiasaura* (my-uh-SOR-uh) in western Montana. The name *Maiasaura* means "good mother reptile." Because some of the nests contained partially grown youngsters, some scientists believe that *Maiasaura* parents may have fed and protected their offspring.

Maiasaura dinosaurs lived during the Cretaceous period. Scientists have discovered a site that contains the fossilized bones of more than ten thousand *Maiasaura* that died after a huge volcanic eruption 80 million years ago. Evidently these animals congregated in large herds and they may have migrated together to find food. Discoveries like this one and the nesting ground suggest that dinosaur behavior was much more complex than we had previously imagined.

(Above left) *Protoceratops* hatchling.
(Above right) A titanosaur hatchling.
(Below) *Maiasaura* hatchling.

(Above) Fossil titanosaur eggshell.

(Below) The sculpted eggshell below is modeled closely on the fossil original.

Among the last dinosaurs that lived on earth were huge, long-necked plant eaters called titanosaurs. The name *Titanosaurus* (ty-TAN-uh-SOR-us) means "giant reptile," and these were among the biggest dinosaurs that ever lived. One species of titanosaur had a forelimb nearly 10 feet long, and another made footprints 3 feet wide. Fossils of titanosaurs have been found in many parts of the world, especially in the Southern Hemisphere.

Nests of titanosaur eggs often occur in groups and suggest that these dinosaurs may have nested in large colonies in the same way that penguins and other sea birds do today. Usually there were about eight eggs in each nest. Stephen's sculpture of a titanosaur nest helps us to picture what such a colony might have been like in dinosaur times.

A young titanosaur emerges from its egg.

The last dinosaur walked on earth 65 million years ago. What we know about dinosaurs today comes from studying their fossilized teeth and bones, skin impressions, eggs, nests, and sometimes even their footprints. Fossil remains of plants and other animals also help us to learn about life in the dinosaur age.

Our understanding of dinosaurs grows and changes as we obtain new information about them. The work of paleoartists helps us envision many of these new ideas. It also helps us to understand and appreciate these extinct reptiles and to resolve questions about what they were really like. As we view sculptures like those of Stephen Czerkas, we are transported into that ancient world, and, for a moment, we can imagine ourselves living in dinosaur times.

Stephen Czerkas views his *Styracosaurus* model.

INDEX

Page numbers in *italics* refer to illustrations.